MW00511279

Stock Market

Investing

An Amazing Guide About Stocks on Margin and Penny Stocks, Including Some Wonderful Strategies That Will Help You in the World of the Stock Market

Written By

Joe Bear

monetary loss due to the information herein, either directly or indirectly.

Respective authors own all copyrights not held by the publisher.

The information herein is offered for informational purposes solely, and is universal as so. The presentation of the information is without contract or any type of guarantee assurance.

The trademarks that are used are without any consent, and the publication of the trademark is without permission or backing by the trademark owner. All trademarks and brands within this book are for clarifying purposes only and are the owned by the owners themselves, not affiliated with this document.

Table of Contents

Introduction

The stock market has generated great impact in recent generations, considered one of the most important markets in the financial world. Attracting millions of people eager to trade online, thanks to the profitability that the stock market generates when using the appropriate strategies, being able to incur in it without the need of having a lot of capital through leverage, an element used by many traders.

But, in order to use it correctly, it is necessary to know the limitations it has, such as the well-known margin. So, what is the margin?

In trading, even if a trader does not have a great amount of resources to invest, it does not mean that he cannot aspire to the high positions of the market, for this, the trading leverage intervenes. A kind of debt contract where the broker grants a certain amount of capital to the trader so that he can fulfill an order to enter the market, using the resources at his disposal. The margin in trading is the deposit that the trader must make in order to open a position in the market, while using leverage.

The margin in trading represents the limit amount that the broker requires to maintain the operation in the market and thus protect himself from losses. When this margin is exceeded by at least 50% of its amount, the broker will issue a margin call, warning the broker to increase the margin in trading or to mobilize the operation in order not to continue losing. If this does not happen, the broker will close the operation promptly to prevent further price decline.

Penny stocks are not suitable for all investors, even though they have many excellent attributes. They can really turn a small investment into a large sum of money fairly quickly (but they can wipe out those dollars just as quickly).

Penny Stocks, those priced at less than five dollars per share, are likely to be companies that have fallen on hard times or are start-ups. Investors are signaling, through the stock price, that they have doubts that the company is sound. If they had no such doubts, the share price would be higher.

But if these companies have shares on the major U.S. exchanges, then they are demonstrating that they have sufficient resources and market knowledge to attract investors, and there is a chance that they will change their business prospects. Successful penny stock investors know that what they should be looking for are signs of a business turnaround.

From these basic concepts, we can move on to the topics we want to discuss in this book, such as: Buying Stocks on Margin, Penny Stocks and Common Strategies to Follow. The goal is to give you enough nourishment to get you started in the world of the stock market at full speed!

I hope you enjoy the book *Stock Market Investing for Beginners: An Amazing Guide About Stocks on Margin and Penny Stocks, Including Some Wonderful Strategies That Will Help You in the World of the Stock Market* to the fullest!

I wish you a good reading!

Chapter 1: Buying Stocks on Margin

You might want to make a trade, but maybe you don't have the money to do it. This is fine, as many brokers will enable you to buy stocks marginally. Margin-buying is a simple concept. To pay for a trade you wish to complete, you borrow money from a broker. You're going to be using that money to buy more stock shares. You could also use the money to access a very expensive stock you couldn't normally afford. Margin trading is a risky strategy, and it's so risky that you might not be able to make a margin account with some investment brokers unless you have a history with that broker. To properly know how margin trading works, you must follow a couple of specific rules.

1. You will need to apply for a margin account to get started. A margin account differs from that of a cash account.

2. You must also sign a margin agreement and agree to the terms for margin trading, which a broker set. This should include information about how large a trade margin can be and what the trade rate is.

3. You can do a deal. You could have $20,000 in a margin account, for example. You might see a stock valued at $400 per share. You might ask to buy that stock from 100 shares. That would need $40,000, though.

4. The amount of money in your account will go toward the part of the cost after you make the trade, while the rest is a broker's loan.

5. At some point, you'll need to pay back the total value of that loan. That will include margin-rate interest. That makes it all the more important to look at that stock's performance. You can always

sell the stock at the right time and cover the loan and interest costs. This only works when you step into a successful position.

6. You'll also need totals to your margin. Your margin account may have certain limits on what you are able to borrow at a time.

Margin Rates

The margin rate is the interest charged on a loan from a broker. Going back to the previous example, you might have been given a 7 percent rate on a margin of $20,000. That means you'll have to pay an interest of $1,400 on the margin trade. The rate is determined by the broker which you are using. For example, for people who deposit less than $25,000 into their margin accounts, Charles Schwab has a margin rate of 8.575 percent. That number is reduced to 7.075 percent for $100,000 accounts and then to 6.825 percent for $250,000 or more accounts. Merrill Edge charges 9,625 percent for $25,000 or less accounts and $100,000 for 7,125 per cent.

The good news about margin trading is that usually, you can borrow up to 50 percent of the total value of the position you want to enter. This is the maximum, which is typical. New margin traders should be able to borrow about 25 percent of their portfolio total. A new trader with a budget of $20,000 could buy about $5,000 in margin-processed trades. Often this limit is used because a person may not have enough margin trading experience. The broker who offers this deal just keeps the risk under control. It's becoming easier to do more with more buying power. You may be given a higher total margin to work with as you have more money in your account, and you continue to be profitable with margin trades. That can get you to the 50 percent value you're aiming for. You might try to buy $10,000 in stock, for example. You may have $5,000 you want to use in cash to pay for the investment. The other amount could be an offer on the margins.

A margin trading company could have limits on how much money you can spend on the trade. For example, you might need to have $15,000 or more in an account to trade in $10,000 on a margin trade. Such rules are applied by trading firms to ensure that people have the necessary funds to carry out trades and repay the loan and any margin-related charges if the trade goes south.

Examples

The following are examples for both again on a margin trade and a loss.

When a Gain Occurs

1. You have a $30,000 Margin Account.

2. You see a stock you would like to buy, but you need to use a margin. In particular, you want to get $150 worth of 100 shares of stock trading. You'd have to spend 15,000 dollars on commerce. For a margin trade, you can always use a part of your $30,000.

3. You are going to have to spend $7,500 on initial trade, and the other $7,500 is going to be on the margin. The margin would have a 7.5 percent interest rate. The interest rate again varies depending on the broker and how much you have put into your margin requirement.

4. When you decide to sell the trade, the stock increases to $190 in value. That $15,000 investment now has a value of $19,000.

5. Along with interest on the loan, you must repay the $7,500 margin. In this example, the interest would be $562.50.

6. From this trade, you'll have made a profit of $3,437.50. The profit is based on how the value of your original $7,500 grew to $9,500. The interest would be withdrawn from commerce. You'll have realized a substantial profit in the end.

This particularly illustrates how, when you work with a margin, you could get a greater profit from a successful trade. Just 50 shares of stock would have been a trade like this without margin. The $7,500 you are investing would turn into $9,500. You would have earned $2,000 from this trade, but that's far less than you'd realized if you'd used a margin trade involving more shares. This is why so many people love to trade margins. They love it is a practice that gives them a greater chance of making a bigger profit than using their own money.

When a Loss Occurs

Obviously, you need a margin trade to be successful in making a profit. The losses that could result from trade-in margins if the stock does not increase in value.

1. You paid $200 for 100 shares of a stock with $10,000 coming from your own account and $10,000 coming from a margin loan. This would also include an interest rate of 7.5 percent.

2. Before you sell the shares, the stock goes down to $150

3. You'll only realize $15,000 if you sell the shares.

4. You must pay back the margin loan of $10,000 plus the interest charge of $750.

5. That results in a $4.250 loss.

Now let's say you went with a straight cash transaction in which you got 50 shares without using a margin for purchasing 100 shares. You'll invest $10,000 in the stock and then sell it to $7,500 for a $2,500 loss. If you spent more money on your margin trade, the potential for you to lose money could be even worse. What is more, if the stock falls further, the damage would be even worse.

For Which Stocks Can You Use Margins?

Please be advised that with each stock, you cannot use margin trades. You can't use margin trades on initial public offerings, penny stocks, or other stocks that could be considered highly risky.

The Board of the Federal Reserve determines which stocks may be marginally tradable. The Board will decide how those stocks are to be used based on various factors, such as how much money is involved, among other factors. The Board's aim is to prevent investors from spending too much money on risky inventories.

Margin Calls

Margin calls are used when the value of stock spikes when you want more cash available. If a stock is making a dramatic decrease, you may need to pay more cash or stock to cover the losses involved. In the meantime, if the price has a huge positive spike, you might be asked to pay the broker back. This is to allow the broker to have the funds available on short notice for managing the trade.

A margin call's total value should be about 10-20 percent of the total investment. That does not mean that there is absolutely going to be a margin call. The best strategy to use here is to look at how the stock has moved and looked at any case where the stock has experienced a dramatic fall in value.

Strategies for Margin Trading

Margin trading is a great way to make more money, but it is only experienced traders who should make margin trades. The potential for a profit could be enormous, but the margin involved can also aggravate any loss you encounter. You can use a few margin trading strategies to keep potential losses from becoming a burden. These focus more on keeping a sense of control.

Keep Your Margins Small at the Start

Just because you could at the beginning get twice the size of an investment when using a large margin trade doesn't mean that's the best idea. You must keep your margins in check whilst at the start using your own money. For example, in the beginning, you can stay with a 10 percent margin. This keeps the danger of a margin trade lower while providing you with a sensible introduction to how those trades work. A smaller trade margin is best when the stock that you want to trade is slightly more unstable. A stock that can change in value in less than a week by 10 percent or more should only be purchased with smaller margins.

Look for Stop Orders

For margin trades, stoppage orders are even more important. You can use a stop order to keep the failures down, but looking at how such orders work for-profits might be even more important. It is best to add a stop order a little over your stock's original value, as this ensures that any margin calls that might occur are minimized.

Avoid Speculation

It's also critical that when looking at what might actually occur with a stock, you avoid any kind of speculation. Speculation is problematic in that it makes an emotional decision easier for a person. This expects a stock to possibly move up in value without actually looking at various factors linked to the stock history.

High Rewards Mean Higher Risks

Although you can understand a profit from your marginal trades, as you would have been able to buy more stocks, this is still a very risky endeavor. As with any type of investment, when the reward is also great, the risk is greater. Because you trade on the margin, you work with more shares than you might otherwise have been able to buy. You are expanding your buying ability, but you also risk losing money.

In short, margin trades are exciting because they can give you a better chance of making a big profit. You also need to watch the value of a stock carefully and how it could change as the losses could be even worse.

Review with the broker you wish to use the terms of the margin trades.

Chapter 2: Penny Stocks

The stocks you read about here are the ones that are expensive to invest in. You don't need to stay with those expensive inventories. You are given the option to select penny stocks. Penny stocks are stocks of firms trading at very low values. The SEC says a penny stock is worth less than $5 per share and will not be listed on one of the major exchanges. Penny stocks sound interesting on the surface because they are so cheap. At the same time, these investments are risky and difficult to work with, because when you trade them, it's impossible to figure out where they might go. There are some things that you can do to successfully trade them out.

What Is a Penny Stock?

A penny stock is a stock with a very tiny market cap. Besides having shares of less than $5 each, the company's market cap is worth about $50 million to $300 million and is not necessarily a globally recognized group. There are also some smaller markets where the stock trades. Penny stocks are traded over the counter in the US. That is, the trades are managed without exchange between the parties. Both the OTC Bulletin Board and Pink Sheets list information on how to organize these penny stocks. The most notable feature of penny stocks is that their values are very small. Some of those stocks may not even be worth one centime per stock.

The small real estate company Metro spaces, for example, trades as an OTC stock under the symbol MSPC. Metro spaces had been trading at $0,0001 per share at the beginning of 2018. Not all penny inventories are so cheap. Another OTC stock with the POTN symbol, Pot network

Holdings, is a stock of a company dedicated to hemp products. The business has a stock that traded at around 50 cents per share for much of 2018.

The general thing about penny stocks is they're very inexpensive. As you will read next, however, these inventories are extremely risky.

Serious Risks

Hard to Prepare Trades

Many investment brokers aren't going to work with penny stocks, believing they're overly risky and hard to find. They may also be struggling with planning orders because the markets involved are slower than the larger ones. There's also the concern about what happens when a single trade shifts stock value.

No Real Standards

Although many stocks have strong standards of how they are to be traded, in penny stocks, you won't find those. Such a stock doesn't have to meet any significant standards to enter an exchange. An OTC penny stock has no information to file with SEC. The OTCBB does ask that the stocks it lists file with the SEC, but this is not particularly necessary. You can still check the SEC to see if there are proper filings for a stock you want to invest in, but that can be hard to find.

Hard to Find Information

The next issue surrounding OTC penny stocks is that you may not get sufficient details about what's available. You won't find much information about penny stocks, as news agencies won't report about them. These firms are too small to actually take some of these news agencies seriously.

You may want to read information about penny stock tips to check out, including stocks that might fascinate people to invest in. Those reports are often made by people who have positions in those stocks, with heavily biased information. They may also give you symbols and names, but not enough information about what you might expect from those stocks to be realizing. That makes it more difficult for you to actually get the details you need. What is even worse is that it is not easy to access those stocks through a website. If you've tried to type "OTC stock quotes" into a search box, you might just come across a bunch of topics listing details on those quotes. This only helps make penny stocks more unreliable due to the lack of information available in the process.

Do You Know the Businesses Involved?

Check out the Pink Sheets to see some of the currently listed businesses. Recognize any one of these? 've you heard about Nutate Energy Holdings before? What about the holdings of Pazoo or Textmunication? Until now, the odds are you've never even heard of these groups.

Figuring out what makes these businesses tick could be a challenge. When you enter a Pazoo search, you will not see the company's website as the first listing on pazoo.com. Instead, you'll see a bunch of links to sites listing information about how the Pazoo stock works on the market and what trends might be noticed in this penny stock. It would take you a while to figure out that this is a wellness and health group which sells online nutritional products.

This is one of the biggest concerns you need to be aware of regarding investing in penny stocks. While penny stocks may seem intriguing, it's almost impossible to figure out what's popular with the stock or why its value might change.

Easy to Inflate or Adjust

Have you ever noticed cases where a penny stock's value has undergone a dramatic shift within a very short time? For example, Reach Messaging Holdings, an OTC stock underneath the RCMH ticker, experienced a significant, very short-lived bump in its value in February 2018. The value of the stock was $0.0003, but it soon moved to $0.0008. It then went down in just one day to $0.0003, and eventually to $0.0002.

What if, at this point, you had a million shares in RCMH? You might have bought them when the stock was $0.0008 believing the stock would continue to rise. You'd spent $800 on the stock. With that stock falling back to $0.0003, you'd have lost $500 on your capital expenditure. Simply put, you went with the conviction that the stock would continue to rise in value, but that stock actually sagged out.

That RCMH stock could have increased in value because there was a massive trade in that stock by one person. That person may have bought 10 million or more RCMH shares and then sold them off in a couple of hours or days after a sizeable increase in the stock. Even worse, that person could be somebody from within the company. This is a legitimate penny stock problem that many people don't even think about. It just takes one person to inflate or deflate a stock's value. This, in fact, often happens with inventories that are not very liquid. A stock that does not have liquidity will not change much in value unless one individual manages to place a huge order and get a considerable number of shares sold or bought all at once.

Pumping and Dumping

A related issue is the pump and dump strategy with which penny stocks often struggle. Although it isn't illegal, it certainly feels like it should be because it manipulates the value of a penny stock directly and is often done by someone from within the business, such as:

1. A person buys a significant number of shares in a stock. Usually, this is for penny stocks, although theoretically, it could happen with any stock. Many penny stocks lacking volume makes them more likely to be targeted by pump and dump schemes. They manipulate much easier.

2. That person then tries to promote a stock by offering false or potentially misleading statements regarding the ability of the stock to grow. In the past, this was done by phone using cold calling techniques. People can now go to social media or create their own topic writing to promote those stocks.

3. Then people fall for those statements and buy the stock. Usually, the people who choose to buy those stocks are willing to invest in them without thinking twice. They could be emotionally driven to invest in those stocks and not thoroughly investigate the company.

4. The person who started the scheme will sell off his shares after enough people buy the stocks in question because that person will have made enough money from the people buying the stock.

5. The people who fell from this trick for the pump and dump scheme could lose hundreds or even thousands of dollars. There are very significant problems with the pump and dump scheme.

What if You Do Want to Invest?

You can still invest, if you wish, in penny stocks. The risks of doing so are high, but it doesn't mean they need to be out of bounds. In fact, if you use a few basic strategies, you could earn money from penny stocks or at least reduce the risks involved. Alongside some more in-depth strategies, many of those are common-sense measures.

Do Not Pay Attention to Success Stories

Have you ever come across some site talking about penny stocks and hear someone report he or she has made tens of thousands of dollars in penny stocks trading? This sounds like a great suggestion and encourages you to invest in those stocks. The truth is, success stories like these, as exciting as they are, are often not legitimate. People who claim they made big bucks on penny stock trading are in the absolute minority. These are people who simply went through a few lucky streaks. Knowing what to find in a penny stock is, of course, critical if you are to succeed. There are so many risks and issues on the market, luck is sometimes more important than simply looking up information about what's available on the market. So you should never assume that these success stories will come true for you.

Don't Hold Penny Stocks Too Long

Decide how long your penny stocks will last. You never know when something will change at any given time and can quickly shrink in value.

Look at how stock in Glance Technologies has changed over time. Around the beginning of 2018, GLNNF had a value of $1.40, but in about two months, that stock fell fast to 60 cents.

Many people buy massive quantities of shares in penny stocks, and it's no surprise that people might experience significant losses. After all, many could buy a large number of penny stocks because they're cheap, and more needs to be bought to make a decent profit. If someone holds a stock too long, that person is at risk of having massive drops in the value of the stock.

Buying and selling a penny-stock the same day is perfectly fine. No matter what you do, avoid holding that stock for more than a few days. There's always a chance you'll lose more than you could earn. The lowest stocks should always have a minimum holding time.

When to Sell?

A good strategy for selling penny stocks is to sell them when you have a 20 or 30 percent return. For example, buying 100,000 shares of a stock at $0.01 and then selling them at $0.012 is great, as you go from a total of $1,000 to $1,200. This is an ideal return of 20 percent. Some investors may hold the stocks assuming a stock could really move forward. Someone could assume the same stock will move up to $0.01 at $0.1. Investing in the stock would be extremely difficult to go from $1,000 to $10,000. Even if it did, this would take a very long time to happen. Of course, when they reach a 20 or 30 percent gain threshold, smart investors will have sold their shares anyway, making it nearly impossible for the stock to actually make that huge increase.

On a related note, you should try to add a stop command to your transaction to prevent potential losses from becoming a threat. Then again, some brokerage firms might not actually offer such orders on penny stocks due to the extended risk associated with them. The risk of a pump and dump event might make it so that the actual value goes well beyond what your stop order was for; at that time, you don't want to have a stop order at $0.1 only for the stock to drop to $0.06.

Watch Company Information

Some firms might claim their stocks are growing well. Company management may, however, skew its documents toward the more positive things about a stock. Some of the positive stories might also be inflated to make them sound more interesting and valuable than they really are. Companies are not necessarily required to tell you about their stocks, certain things. They could be working very hard to make their stocks more intriguing for you without revealing any real substance. Always take whatever a company says about its stock and how it changes with a grain of salt, so you don't fall into any investment traps.

Choose Stocks With a High Volume

The next tip is to stay with stocks that have a good volume of trading. These are the inventories people actually buy. These could include stocks traded by a lot of people, thereby reducing the risk of a stock pump and dump scheme. Everything that has at least 100 million trading volumes is always worthwhile. That means that within the last 24 hours of trading, at least 100 million shares were traded.

That tip has one major caveat. You need to look at how the volume changes for a penny stock, based on what is shown in the read-out chart. A chart, for example, could show one or two massive spikes in a stock price. That means one person controlled a great deal of trading. It could, of course, be a sign of a pump and dump attack as well.

It is always easier to trust any stock with a graph or chart that is a little more variable and doesn't have lots of odd shifts in its value.

Avoid Trading More Than Needed

The specific number of penny stock shares that you can purchase could be limitless. While you might be motivated to purchase one million stock shares at a value of $0.0005, that could be a serious risk, in fact. You'd spend $500 on an investment that, if you're not careful, could be going south rather quickly.

On the contrary, try to keep your penny stock holdings from being worth more than a hundred dollars. A better idea is to stay with 100,000 shares at $0.0005. You would only spend $50 on your trade, but at least you won't lose a lot of money if the stock decreases rather than growing as you anticipated.

Never Sell Short

When you think about it, the sale of short sounds like a great idea. You can borrow penny stock shares that appear to have been pumped up, sell them, and then buy back those stocks for a sizeable profit. The truth is that you could lose so much money from the trade than you could afford. For a penny stock, the time period for a short sale could be far too long.

Review Your Position

Consider how your position is organized based on the size of the volume of the stock. Never trade more than 10 percent of the volume of that stock. If you did that, you would end up inflating the stock price. Investing far too much at one time only adds to the overall transaction risk involved. When getting this part of the trade organized, you need to be careful.

When working with penny stocks, remember that you are fully aware of what you're going into in the process. If you are not careful, such stocks could prove to be dangerous and harmful to your investment plans.

Chapter 3: Common Strategies to Follow

We're going to speak about some of the more popular tactics that certain people may have learned about, even though they're not particularly acquainted with the equity market's workings.

Buying On Down Days

In general, that is not a terrible thing. The broker calls you up and advises you that there appears to be a down day on the street, and it may be a smart opportunity to pick up any stocks at the low.

As you'll have come to know, when it comes to capital market activity there are still two sides of a coin.

If you're someone with a strong market analysis system that focused your investment decisions on sound facts and numbers, then a down day might potentially be a moment when you might want to pick up any stocks you've purchased at a lower price. Also, a down day doesn't imply you're wasting any of your money on those better cost products. The astute investor will drive the positions in sections more frequently than not, with the expectation that a down day might quite well turn out to be a down week. That will indicate decent rates for products picking up.

However, if you are merely betting on the tips and calls of the broker, a splurge into the market on a down-day could become a cause for depression if the market doldrums continue over the week or even a month. You just purchased it, you figured it was a decent deal, and now it's gone down much more.

Buying on down days cannot be seen as a tactic alone but as part of a well-planned framework as a whole. There is, nevertheless, a claim that purchasing on down days may be a tactic too, and here is how it goes.

You buy on a day off. If the price drops more down the next day, you pay exactly what you paid. Then if the price drops more down the following day, you repeat the prior day's sales again. You'd only made seven multiples of the original first-day purchase at this point.

You then pursue this buy if the downward go on before there is a rebound that the market price does not fall below the day before, and so you sell it all off.

Since you've acquired product in higher numbers at cheaper rates, you've basically downgraded the expenses, and thus, when there's a market spike, selling off anything can be a benefit net.

The difficulty with this is the requirement to provide large quantities of money to continue the endless purchasing. Imagine something occurring for 15 days, how many multiples will it have been? Not something I'd suggest, so it's not worth the risk-benefit ratio to me.

Dollar-Cost Averaging

This is because many investment analysts and citizens are moving the shares and exchange-traded securities (ETFs)

Are you really trying? The basic principle is that you designate a date, claim the first day of the month to dive into the financial instruments in your currency, regardless of the market fluctuations that day. You're here.

Then do this regularly over the following months, with the period chosen over putting the capital into investing per the first day of the month.

You basically take out of scenario the timing of the market or actually randomize the timing of the market. By adding funds per month on a particular day in the period, you neglect the market dynamics at that moment of time in merely concentrate on reaching your roles.

Financial analysts prefer this concept because it makes the assets of the clientele easy to handle. Of note, the dollar cost measure, under such circumstances, still has its merits. It is our job to know what these requirements are and how the overall cost of the dollar can be exploited for our gain.

Generally speaking, when the economy is a rising trend, getting a set sum to spend on a given date would mean that you are only buying fewer units at a better price.

The same would be valid when the demand is downward heading, where the set volume will then cause a greater buying quantity at a lower price.

The average cost to most folk would be the commercial appeal of the dollar, the fact that it looks like an idiot-proof way to invest. Think about it; you're setting aside a comfortable sum per month or annum, or whatever period you choose. Then you literally plunge it into the stock or stocks that you have picked. More frequently than not, though, you will drive that into mutual funds or exchange-traded funds since they are, in reality, investments that are investing in various securities and properties, and so you believe that might be best for liquidity and stability.

For me, whether you intend to participate in the equity market and its relevant capital services, time should never be removed from the table entirely. Why? Why?

People who blissfully have dollars take an average of one year or even two to three years can have half or a tonne of their financial worth washed away only because they choose to participate in a bear market because their prevailing plan was to go long or buy stocks.

If one truly decided to sell or invest like an ostrich, so at least seven to fourteen years would need to be the minimum horizon. This is such that you can view yourself in two simultaneous economic cycles and thereby have a subsequent effect on the capital markets.

To me, the average cost of the dollar has its benefits, but you need to understand how to do it and, most specifically, to determine if it is really acceptable for your specific do. This sort of investing plan will be perfect for people who have limitless stamina, have a decent career or extra cash flow every month rolling in and don't even get concerned by the sums they're plugging into the markets. The crux of the matter is that they can spend a sum they feel really happy with and that they would rarely not have to change the level of money even in the direst emergencies.

These people would profit from this approach because it suits them fairly well because they actually don't have a crippling curiosity even on a weekly basis in researching the financial markets. While their earnings are good, they would find it exceedingly challenging to overtake timers in the sector. I tell this honestly and based on what I heard and learned. It does not knock on the cost balancing technique of the dollar at all.

Like I said earlier, there are numerous roads leading to Rome, and everyone has their favorite route.

Indeed, the overall expense of the dollar may be perceived as a stand-alone tactic, albeit a very simplified one. However, those who wish to reap full profits from it will need to monitor and timing the sector, and others who only want to make their capital function better for them without suffering through problems would also need to consider a longer keeping duration or horizon.

Bear Market Strategy

This is basically a purchase on bad days' situation derivation. Generally, bear markets are known as such after the economy has experienced a drop of twenty percent in stock prices or where the stocks have been exposed to sustained downward pressure for several months or even years.

For me, bear markets can have numerous and varying mathematical metrics to decide by, so a rather easy approach is to head out into the streets and start talking to people you're accustomed to seeing on a regular basis. Taxi drivers, restaurant waiters, and maybe also primary school instructors! If neither of them would like to chat with you about the equity market, you're potentially in the money if you put your bet that the economy is definitely in the doldrums and the sector is somewhat bearish.

Everyone becomes a financial market whiz when the shares are optimistic, and that is where the word irrational exuberance introduces itself. By comparison, when no one tries to give their well-meaning suggestions about which stocks to buy or sell, and when even the stock market whisper will bring people into jitters or advise them to keep away, then you definitely realize that the bear market is on its way.

The solution for the bear market is also fairly basic. Simply define the bear market era accurately, and

What you do need now, though, is trust. And when other people are huddled at home with their cash fund collections, you'll head out into the street to purchase products.

Creating your confidence would require a clear and strong study of the firms that are piquing your attention, but still ensuring that you do not overestimate yourself in the department of capital. Sell markets may be reasonably brief, although others can be reasonably deep, which is why the confidence of remaining engaged is necessary to understand the opportunity for benefit.

These sorts of scenarios do not exist on a regular or weekly basis, but it would be fair to assume that those concerned with day trading or short-term swing trading wouldn't have anything to do here. The bear market plan is really about people who normally have cash on hand, because they've done their homework in such a way that when the moment arrives they're beyond doubt and can behave in trust when they're backed up by anyone else.

One quirk is that others would also mix the method of cost averaging the currency with this tactic for the bear market. This involves foresight and confidence that the bear market is still on us, and then a clear scheme can be formulated to trigger regular stock and fund sales while the markets begin to fall. Some prefer this as opposed to trying to plunge in larger amounts in one go, while some tend to hold to their calculations and focus their investments on price ranges that they have determined to be of worth.

Again I would claim in both situations, there is no right or wrong. Most notably, a reasonable match for the customer needs to be the approach. As I would like to suggest, if you earn a hundred thousand dollars but are continuously shivering with anxiety and sweat-drenched, I would rather take advantage of ten thousand to sleep comfortably and without any worries.

The bear market strategy has its position and period for usage, but due to the very existence of being a bear market, it is not ideal for those searching for fast trades. It's a really nice way for me to spend the surplus funds for which you have no need and to sit invested in securities or instruments that can't earn profits for a few years down the line.

Day Trading

This used to be a fad because I was already battling the market. At this point in time, I believe it to always be. Many day-trading advocates will claim it's one of the easiest ways to sell and get wealthy. In the afternoon you reach and leave both of your places. You scout your stocks and plan them throughout the day. Within the trading time period, you make all your choices, and so after the market ends, you are a happier individual, and you will go to bed with no fears, unlike others that have current securities.

All this is well and dandy, but as I have already said, there will always be two sides to everything with respect to the stock market.

If you lock yourself up and only be willing to exchange within the time span of a day, what happens if you don't have any decent trades to pick from? Do you believe you'd have the opportunity to indulge in a transaction, or you would not really gain money for the day? What occurs if the condition of this sort of exchange is less than one day, two days, or even three days in a row? Could you guess how much tension and anxiety the day trader has to endure at this juncture? The day trader may therefore be compelled to participate in a deal that may not be the most desirable to get out of this. That represents an enhanced loss risk.

The typical counter-argument to this will be that the world of stocks, as well as financial instruments, is so large that at least one decent trade would certainly be set up every day. The world may be large, but your resources will restrict the degree to which you would comfortably evaluate the stocks you choose to sell. There is just so much that artificial intelligence and computerized aids will achieve, with the human brain also required for deeper research.

The other part of day trading where you have to remember will be on the benefit side. Tell you sold a portfolio for the day. Twenty points in the day went up, and you've happily banked with the income. It holes out the following day, when the market exchange only opens at a far higher price than the closing price of the previous day. This kind of scenario occurs when there are good reports from overnight or when the purchasing desire is too strong.

As a day trader, anytime some kind of upward sprint occurs, you are pushed into the periphery. You may be able to fall into the act and just leap through the structures and laws, and that will be the first move to foolishness.

Day trading is almost of an opportunistic practice to me. If there is an optimal time to do so, we can do it. It's really much about how they used to do hunting and fishing – in seasons. When the season is perfect for day trading, we can do so because it really does increase your sharpness and contribute to your benefit capacity. We should have our other structures and strategies to focus on when the season isn't there. Trading on the day doesn't work all the time, so it is another useful weapon in the arsenal when it can be put to use.

One note of advice, however, to get the hang of day trading, you will have to learn more. This is attributed to the demands for pace and rapid decision-making, as well as the requirement for strong analytical skills. Often you could hear folks claim they're dealing from the gut, or they just felt like they had to get out of storage. Take them with a grain of salt, and dig into it further. Possibly these guys have had plenty of experience coping with the market or the specific product, which is why they are willing to operate on their whims and fancies, obviously. In reality, their brains have absorbed the knowledge they need, and then they can make the choices very easily.

Shorting

This side of the market carries a certain fascination and allure to certain folks, since about 50 percent of consumers are now mostly acquainted with the fact that stocks can only be acquired. They don't understand the idea that, according to trading terms and conditions, you can potentially sell short stocks that you don't buy.

Usually, short selling will enable you to sell quickly from a selection of stocks made accessible by the brokerage. This is because these are stocks that are held by the company or have received authorization from stock owners to accept borrowing. Short sellers will also be allowed to sell their non-owned securities, but would have to pay interest for the day their short positions remain operating. This same paying attention goes as we are even concerned for conditional contracts. (MFF)

Shorting as a tactic is once again part of the game that you may apply to your arsenal. Imagine the stock market situation where the bear market is just beginning. You realize that the price is going to drop by 20 percent or more, and if you have the opportunity to shorten those picked products, why not make a profit on the way down until you make the reversal and start buying the products on the cheap one?

Is it always important that you have to learn shortcut? I'd agree it's nice to know, and it's a safe choice to have available, but to be competitive in capital markets, it's not a must-have.

Taking the situation on the bear market that we spoke about earlier. If you didn't have the opportunity or simply didn't like shorting, you'd simply keep out of the market before the bear market sales kicked in and you began your long positions in your preference stocks. In the meantime, what will you do as the economy went down, you ask? You might be quietly sitting on cash doing nothing, or you could be trading in other sectors. Not all stocks work in unison, and as one is in the early stages of a bearish period, another may flow into the start of a bull run.

One thing I feel obliged to claim will be that short-term benefit appears to be higher. Exactly what do I mean?

If you were a stock too low at a certain point and you had the right call, the downward trend would typically be even smoother than if you were on the same call with the very same stock for a long time. This is why shorting income typically come far sooner than longing income.

This stems from two primary impulses, covetousness and anxiety. In the case of shorting, the prevailing emotion that can be found on the stock exchange is anxiety. When a stock takes a dive, most committed people will not be willing to bear the impact and will want to get out fast. Their ultimate philosophy will not be to waste their capital in the stock anymore.

When we get a product that goes up in price, speculation is the biggest reason people come and drive the profit up in order that they will offer it at a better profit later on. Greed has a driving power marginally lower than terror because the human mind still needs to preserve what it has first. It cannot withstand everything it holds from separation. Therefore the fear of losing still trumps the reward greed.

That's just something you ought to take care of, but it's not a clarion call for you to leap on the shorting bandwagon anyway. I repeat that it is nice to recognize, but it is by no way sufficient for the financial markets to perform well.

Penny Stocks

When this technique really came into dominant action, I'm not aware, but to be frank, I never really used it actively. It doesn't mean I didn't take penny stock positions, but it does mean I didn't launch those positions only because they were penny stocks.

This approach relies primarily on small stocks, which are comparatively inexpensive in contrast with the more mainline stocks in play. When you take a stake in a penny stock, you will get thousands or even tens of thousands of them. The entire theory will be to wait in the market action for a tick up and then by dint of value, you are simply selling out the penny stock shares to cash in some gains.

A change of the penny stock approach will be to reach a few markets that you perceive to be positive and then buy positions of penny stocks that belong to certain businesses. This time around, the investment of penny stock wouldn't be huge, so you'd be looking for a bigger price change to understand the opportunity for benefit.

My positions in penny stocks mostly came into existence after I evaluated the stock, and I certainly didn't have the requirements that the stock could be a penny stock first.

For a cause, penny stocks adhere to the group and may vary from something like the poorly managed business to bigger structural stuff such as being in a sunset market. Performance and worth are also not to be used as the market plunge to what is called the bottom of the penny. For instance, the sector may be terribly incorrect on times, or the penny stock business is doing a great rebound.

Much of my penny deals are around the fact that businesses are always known to have any appeal and development prospects, and it is only because of seasonal causes that hammered down the market price that it counts as a penny commodity.

But if I say temporary, it could be either a quick or a long wait. We never do.

As such, in my view, the penny stock investing approach isn't really one that can hold up if the scheme was solely focused on getting the stock requirements to be penny stocks.

For me, that looks so much of a risk and smacks too much expectation. Hoping that every day the stock would go up, or hoping that the market would only fall so that the whole portfolio could be sold for a benefit. If you are in stock market optimism and there is little more to support your continued interest, it should be about time to put the exit order.

Know Yourself

I realize it has been stated before, but in the light of these widely heard investing methods, I would like to hear it once again.

Many of the tactics have their applications, as we have shown. What is more relevant now is to have a clear idea of how the personality for trading is, and then pick certain tactics that you think will be a good match for you.

An individual who dislikes needing to glance at the monitors and continually being bound to the computer will be a bad match for day-trading. An individual who likes relentless action and lives for instant gratification will be a bad match for strategy in the bear market.

There are no perfect size suits all tactics out there, as it is. What would be more realistic would be to gain awareness of the various methods that you find acceptable for yourself and then turn it into a cohesive framework that can be conveniently utilized by you.

Having said that, I would like to define those traditional techniques described above as being what I might consider the tip of the iceberg. We're going to explore the investment analytics schools a bit more in detail later, and it will actually open up deeper into the investment management environment.

Strategy School Of Thought

This section can cause an explosive debate. I'm all set for it because I was selling myself through all fields of learning. This is the controversy over conceptual analyses and scientific research that is ever-present.

Before I move much further, I want to illustrate the importance of research in the field of stock picking. The findings of a well-worked and thorough study are also a building pillar that will help reinforce the judgment in moments where everybody and all is telling the contrary of what you are doing. Research offers you confidence, and you have the steady strength and capacity to ride out the turbulent waters and stop market turbulence with certainty. More specifically, you build your own understanding of stock and market place. That is still priceless. And if you might be mistaken, but the mere fact that you've developed a perspective based on a comprehensive and well-worked framework allows you the freedom to fine-tune and change your business views as the path continues.

Dream of someone who doesn't have a vision of his shoes for a while. Instead, he depends on press stories, stock magazines, and traders to fill him with suggestions of what his next major move might be. Compare it to someone who's qualified to have business understanding and angle. True, he can also collect news and investment notes, and who can claim he can't draw encouragement from these resources to find a decent invitation to stock? The main distinction is that the individual getting taught would do his own screening and a thorough examination to shape his point of view. Then he should equate his interpretation to those portrayed in the material. If divergence is clear, so he will quickly let it go.

This is in comparison to the individual who has little experience. If he's letting go of the order, he'd be concerned if the stock eventually soars to the sky, feeling regretful. And he is still traumatized by each fluctuation in rates even though he is in stock, so he loses confidence.

Proponents of basic and theoretical analyses have been at loggerheads for as long as anybody can recall. -- side strongly insists that their way of thinking is better and therefore inspires people in any path to take up studies.

I may try, for myself, to suggest that my comprehensive schooling was in the context of fundamental research. That means I was qualified in business balance sheet arithmetic and cash flow statements. We also learned to look at the business and assess its valuation so that we can foresee the course of the stock price.

It was enjoyable at school since the figures stagnate equally, and you didn't have to deal with feelings or the financial markets' hustle and bustle. Hypotheses created on paper stayed unchanged and did not alter. Company factors have not been entirely factored in yet. You didn't have cases of corruption or immoral conduct that might have a detrimental effect on market values. It was pretty tidy and sterile, with all.

Folks who believe strongly in quantitative research trust in the idea that the revenue, cash flow accounts, and the balance sheet displayed in the financial results are the key component of the puzzle they will use to break business code. They also belong to the prevailing mindset where they regard stocks as strict firms, and thus their cognitive process will revolve around evaluating the market environment and the like. Industry opportunities and entry hurdles will be at the top of their priorities if there is a decision to purchase or sell a stock.

Fundamentalists perform really well for me because they work in the context of problems that are long-lasting. The empirical bent of looking at a company's economics can take you to a filtration method. You should pick out the very powerful from the obvious ones, whilst at the same time, you might sort others who are not apparently so bad as what the market tends to decide.

As fundamentalists, we should pick out the strong firms because, in the case of some unexpected situations such as corporate abuse or exploitation, the only way is to wait for the stock to comply with the company's standards.

That is also the issue.

Often it takes a couple more times until the business catches on, then you'd be willing to enjoy the profits only for making the right choice. On some occasions, it could take you years or eons. You gladly went in with the money and, in a certain amount of time, anticipated certain benefits, and yet those hopes fall flat. The world also doesn't want to know too well what you should do! At that time, the expenditure is static, and the monies are bottled away, unable to be used elsewhere for a better future return.

In a future where there was somebody with infinite wealth, I think he'd be a really content fundamentalist because he'd be willing to deposit funds in certain businesses he'd find worth the risk and then wait for the moment to develop. Since he has nearly infinite money, he will have no concerns about the potential cost of assets. Naturally, that is the perfect setting. We exist in the modern world, and so we would have little means to name ourselves.

At this juncture, it is here where technical observers step in to point out the obvious shortcomings in the conceptual school of thinking and then rejoice in the strictly tactical trading system's apparent advantages.

At one point in my life, technological trading represented the Holy Grail for me; I was so stuck on it because I always felt that if I just discovered the right technological framework, my life would be set, and my business career would be free.

There are still several sellers of technological systems seeking to react to certain assumptions that getting "the" technical system will reflect prosperity and passive income for all the rest of eternity.

Take it from me. In trade, there is no such thing as a holy grail. In some cases, only technological processes will perform better and recover all the gains and have the losses double in other cycles. Trading algorithms can see returns in certain frames, but in others, they do offer nothing but losses.

This is not meant to break the ego, just to say the facts and what it is. For all those people who clearly claim they trust in the strength of their shifting averages, candlestick trends, and retracements of Fibonacci, you should be fairly confident that there may be more than you can see.

I felt like an energizer bunny when I first began practicing Strategic Trading. The name of the game during those days was Back training. I'd concocted a combination of technical signals and then compare those signals back with a bunch of stocks to see the risk of loss of gain. I did it once non-stop for thirty days, and you know what, the outcome I received was a flat loss rate for a victory. That, of course, did not dissuade me in the least, since I strongly assumed that the issue resides in the concoction of technological signals, not elsewhere. As soon as I managed to create the right balance of technological signals, everything will be fine. So I thought.

It was a few years of humbling and exhausting, and at the end of my rope, as I was almost on the brink of giving up, I chanced across the idea of market action or product volume action analysis as some may term it.

The idea is that all that is to be learned regarding the stock or investment tool has already been recorded in both the price and its movement. In the case of inventories, we even have the secondary regular inventory metric is helpful proof.

This was like a letter given by a deity to one who was approaching the end of his path. It made any sense to me, at last. I didn't have to think too much about stochastics, shifting averages, and Bollinger pairs. (If all these sound like a foreign language to you, just know it doesn't matter) Price and volume will be everything I cared for.

The theory was straightforward and enticing, but in the beginning, it was very difficult when attempting to adapt to the modern world. Regulation on rates was besotted of market increases. Such market ranges were considered to be bands of assistance and opposition, and you were supposed to devise strategies to compensate for occasions when rates plummeted across certain bands or when rates rebounded away from those bands.

I've been tottering down this road for about three years, and frankly, at that point in time, it didn't appear to me I was going anywhere. If you shot a stumbling sailor in a bar struggling to rush away and catch the shuttle, it will be a detailed description of my trading experience on the equity market at the moment. It wasn't until I learned, truly learned and held copious notes of my trade newspapers that I actually made any headway for decent benefit.

My own interpretation and usage of the basic and scientific schools of thinking will ultimately be central to targeting and filtration. I focus on the simple side of things to open up my reach and narrow down can stock I should be involved in. The technical analysis will play its role in deciding where and when the lever to join could be pulled, as well as exiting stock positions. This was a collaboration between the two great homes, and it was a lucrative arrangement that catered my tastes.

I can understand if you feel rather deflated at this stage, or maybe a little interested. Deflated because I have confirmed without a question that there is no holy grail and intrigued about what I have achieved to build the revolution for myself.

I want to repeat the section of not getting a holy grail. I say it's just not my concern if you chose not to accept that and go on splurging thousands of dollars of your hard-earned cash on folk services that try to sell you. I would just point out that if such devices perform too well, the people who market them probably won't allow you to have your hands on them. That is because the technological structures are struggling from what we term the impact of widespread use. If a certain critical mass of citizens decides to operate on the same technological signs, the exchange is essentially annulled. Even even though these devices have not suffered from the consequences of widespread use, why would these people choose to sell them to you for fewer than ten thousand people a day, because they would actually create so much of a day out of these devices?

There's just no free lunch in the world at the end of the day, and if anything seems almost too nice to be true, then it generally is.

Now for the section about my success, short of sending you a personal one on a single coaching session to lead you on what works for me from a professional point of view, it's going to be really challenging to write it down because it works for you too. There are some tips I kept during the climb up, though.

Analysis of the trade journal and create links with market transactions

Reaching at the initial stage of the wider time span. You'd want to venture through the lower time frames just once you have a defined collection of guidelines and structures.

You don't need to rush; there's nothing in the universe who can push you to sell, so just take your time and start the exchange on your terms.

Please make sure to include a list of rules to obey. Even if it's only a one-liner at the outset, create the practice of making guidelines so you'll have limits within which to work.

Some Other Useful Things

I'm going to speak about certain topics in this segment that I think will be very useful to someone who wants to make more money out of trading in the stock market.

Momentum Trading

Trading and trading policy of this type depends strongly on, as the name implies, momentum. In other terms, how we build and conduct this plan will be equally contingent on purchasing or selling interest at present and planned.

Strategies may be as easy as I can commit to joining the stock the next day at the starting price if the stock has had a distance up day. This is attributed to the assumption that the trader hopes to maintain the upward trend, and therefore making such a pass. Related situations may be rendered where there has been a break in the stock down day.

Here the crux of the matter is to recognize the energy that will hopefully continue for at least a few days. A longer time will, of course, be most welcome. Sometimes, people who are only doing momentum-based trading might not have such decent win-loss percentages with their transactions, but will cover up for that with their bigger profit margins. We should not depend entirely on momentum, but rather aim to integrate it into our trading processes.

I use a motivation for the additional boost to pull in the extra money for myself. But in cases when I might have missed my goal benefit for a specific product, if I see traction in the market counter, I can only let the place continue to run.

Recognizing that certain sources of energy waves originate from the press will be the way to distinguish permanent traction from others that may fizzle out easily. Therefore it is our duty to easily and cleverly discern which bits of news have a real effect on the bottom line, and others are all everyday hogwash. Continuing to get the news that has a significant effect on the profit prospects and profitability of the business is very unusual, but we are still looking at and piece of news immediately in relation to our specific stock information. This also assumes the more acquainted you are with stock and business, the easier you'd be separating out actual news from the noise of the economy.

Trend Following

This can be considered a tactic and, at the same time, a common concept that the bulk of traders choose to obey. Trade the trend, pursue the trend, the trend is that your buddy will list among the many terms that make life better for yourself as you exchange and spend in the course of the pattern.

Only imagine it. If you have a product that has a price chart that essentially moves non-linear upward for a very long period of time, it would be fair to say that if your goal was to lengthen the product, you would have a greater chance of winning a deal.

I've been in those circumstances before, and I'll tell you it's essentially quick to only put your orders at the correct technical stage, wait for the stock price to fall back and go up to certain technical prices, and then watch your orders get filled out. After the retracement, when the market continues its upward rise, you stand by to gain a benefit or to control your portfolio positions. Benefit taking may also be an agonizing choice since you tend to lock in gains but at the same time not having to leave so much capital on the table as the stock starts to meteor upwards. Often I do it with a part of the assets gaining benefit and moving my emotional stop losses to break even with my other current section. This basically generates a concept for me that I can see the actual stock portfolios as "free" for the already earned gains charged for purchasing these new stocks. Getting free stocks doesn't imply you should handle them differently, only then there's that little extra room you're allowing yourself to gain a little less or to generate a lot of money. In certain situations, it would typically turn out to be breakeven for this free part, or I am collecting almost twice as much income as if I were trying to cut off all as a whole. My decision to undertake this step relies solely on my stock and business evaluation, as well as the existing technological condition. I would have to confess, of course, that the niggling sensation of taking a chance would typically be the main instigator for me to suggest making this leap, but the determination about whether to do so would always be focused on facts and statistics.

Trading and trading in the movement certainly has its advantages, which is why so many people expound it and even make it their slogan. But it is often challenging to understand and refine into a functioning investment plan.

One of the biggest factors being that you have to be conscious of what span of time you are on as you look at the graph. There are numerous timescales, varying from minute charts to monthly maps. None would disagree with you that the longer the duration, the weightier such price charts will get. This is since an indicator on the month map is a reflection of the market movement for the individual stock over the entire month. The battle of the month between the bulls and the bears, as well as the cumulative total of the money they contributed to the war, are all encapsulated in that month's table. On the other side, a candle on the one-minute map will certainly have far less money invested into it relative to the month list, thereby reducing its confidence amount. Similarly, a pattern on a minute chart might be upward, but you may easily disregard the minute chart while the day chart or month chart is telling a downward tale.

Looking at higher cycle maps, such as day, week, and month levels, are best as you're starting off first. Compared to the longer time spans, the patterns depicted on these maps will have a smaller chance of turning out not to be permanent.

Another issue about pattern investing will be to have reasonable entry and exit locations. Let's say that you've finished your research and found the stock you'd like to pull the lever to enter in its upward trajectory. Currently, it is at $50 per share price. Any people could just pull the trigger and hop in at $50. Others should do what I normally do and park orders at fixed price levels that make us say $30. If the market retraces, which the market normally does, and there are barely any instances of the straight line shooting up or down, so, at a reasonable price, I'll get into stock. This also means I have nothing to risk than a person who goes in at $50 only because my price is, so to say, lower to the "park." In general, when the stock entry price is higher to the bottom, where the bottom implies $0, then you have a more secure location, just like a lower center of gravity in physics rules.

An individual purchasing at $50 or an individual purchasing at $30 will seem different only because of the various entrance rates. The $30 guy will have more leeway to transfer the product. Think about it, if the stock price changes to $40, that's a $10 benefit for the $30 guy but a $10 loss for the $50 consumer. Naturally, a decent dose of strategic research will have to base this company with a sensible entry and exit stage. It is important to chart and decide the entrance and exit points from the technological level, and therefore the next thing to do is to have the mindset of being willing to leave the exchange.

What? What? Had I understood it, right?

Actually, you have finished. Have the emotional preparedness to leave the company. Why do you think so? This is for the occasions where the retracement exists, but it does not reach the stage, which is logically calculated. But instead of falling to $30, it rises to $33, then stages a recovery afterward. This is also valid during occasions where there is no retraction, and the market tends to rumble from $50 onwards.

You do have cases like that. Therefore, you must still be prepared emotionally to let go of the exchange and step on to the next. That is also why the investing and trading framework should never be too limiting to provide either one or two triggers every year. Imagine if you skipped the last trading chance, you might have to wait until next year to have another one.

I would also like to point out that the $50 guy might not actually be incorrect in our case, but it's just my nature to err on the cautionary side. I will tell kudos to him if the $50 guy had the gumption and the money required to handle the possible bumpier trip than the $30 guy might. What I term a "jumper" will be the $50 man. Typically these guys leap into a market out of fear of losing out. Jumpers rule the roost in moments where the movement is roaring, and the press is on the spot, which also has significant structural effects. There's absolutely no place for people who want retracements entry because there's just zero.

You either hop in that kind of circumstance, or you pass on to the next possible stock. Mentality and temperament play a major part in whether you'd be an effective jumper. And we also recognize that the nature of investing is primarily influenced by the volume of cash at stake for any particular moment in time. If you want to train yourself as a jumper and yet find yourself missing the requisite mental criteria, beginning small will be the solution. When leaping, fear tiny quantities before you get used to the sensation of it. You will also be forced to scale up to a reasonable level progressively.

I'm not much of a jumper myself, but I leap when the chance occurs. Jumping is like every other talent in the field of trade and finance, always useful to add to your arsenal so you can rely on it anytime you find you need it.

How can you decide the pattern will be another problem for some people, where others would adhere to the concept of utilizing moving averages to evaluate the pattern, and some might find Bollinger band use to be the only valid way to determine the trend?

After potentially thousands of hours staring at the maps, I've come to know that when the pattern is apparent, it's so clear that you don't require any metrics or new-catched technologies to tell you to claim this is a pattern. The Map visual analysis is what you need. I would prefer to stay on the higher time frame for me and then do a visual analysis to assess what seems like the imminent theme that is actually affecting the sector. Going from top left to bottom right will mean a downward step.

Pattern. Moving from the bottom left to the top right would indicate that the bulls will have power. If you try and search, because you can't find something that's clear, that's what we say by a trendless condition or a side sector. If a market moves sideways, that typically means the fight between the bulls and the bears is going on, and the outcomes are not yet clear.

Sideways markets are perfect circumstances for day trading, by the way, so you have what you imagine is a sort of map in a pretty rectangular type. This ensures that the top and bottom borders are equally established for you to deal with day to day. We won't dive too much into the trading part of this day right now, maybe more in a future novel.

But there's no reason to over-complicate stuff; visual examination typically fits well since it's the easiest because when items are clear, they're generally in the truest shape.

The Need For Stop Losses

This idea was discussed at multiple junctures in this book, but I felt it's worth a segment of its own, only because of its significance in the field of trade and investment.

A stop-loss or a decreased loss is simply a fixed price point that is the escape signal for everybody to get out of a poor deal. The idea of getting a quantity that will be acceptable for the individual person to sacrifice falls into play here.

Tell Adam has decided he's willing to gamble $1000 on a certain sell offer, and he's got a hundred shares now selling at a $40 price point. It will then mean it his stop-loss price point will be at $30 if the trade call is a long one, so his risky $1000 capital would be divided by his hundred shares to produce a $10 price space. His exchange will then have space for a gyrate of up to $30, and if the price point drops below that, then he would close the deal, dust himself off, and then go ahead to the next.

This point is also the section where I would like to highlight the significance of closing the candle or bar on which you are tracking time period ever. If you're a day trader, you might be gazing at the end of the hourly light. That implies if the market price still falls below $30 on every hourly closing light, you'd be conducting the closure of the exchange. If you were a swing or long-term trader, though, you might look at the closing of the day candle or even the closing of the week candle. It would suggest you'd just conduct the exit plan when the market moves and ends on the day or week candle around $30 based on the time period you're monitoring. Keep in mind that regardless of the vast volume of money required to create and fight for the results of that specific candle, the longer the time span, the more confidence it would hold.

This argument would also contribute to another controversial field that has long been subject to discussion. Few people would say that if you chose to adopt this method, the cumulative number of damages that would be sustained would be more than the safe sum that one would spend. This is because as we are waiting for the day or week candle to end, after crashing through the predetermined point, the price may fell even further. Considering the scenario above, you could see rates at $25 or even $20 while your price range was expected to be $30. It will end in a double loss of the money you were able to fork out.

For me, I understand the drawbacks of using the stop loss in this manner, but I prefer to only do things this way because of the benefits things confers. The one big benefit you get by performing the stop loss upon closure will be that you'd be avoided circumstances when the price jumps dramatically up or down, and sometimes it doesn't close at all.

Take Adam and his stock as our example once again. The approved price for stop loss was $30. If his stock swings significantly within the hour, say

$20, and yet he still tries to keep his composure and convince himself to wait until the closing hour, he may notice that at the closing hour, the stock price maybe has rebounded back to $35. And also produces what we term a pin bar or a hammer or what people might deem the candle handle.

What Adam has done by keeping his composure to get out of a condition that might have flushed his lack of stoppage. He's still in the game amid the intra-hour downward shift that turned out to be nothing but a terror.

These conditions may appear in all time frames, but keep in mind that the wider the time span, the more money to devote.

So what to do with the question of getting to pay about exactly what you were able to sacrifice initially? The solution is to transact in limited quantities. Imagine this period for Adam, instead of a hundred shares, he's only exposed to fifty shares because he knows the vulnerability of closing utilizing the stop loss, he's easily circumvented the problem, yet he's still held his safe losing number.

So when I say this, I generally get confronted with some hoots and derision, as some people would then suggest, won't the benefit opportunity be diminished similarly? The response is a yes, of course, and now I would like to inform everybody that it is all first about what you can and are able to sacrifice before we move on worrying about benefits and benefits. If we can maintain a solid basis on our expenses, so of course, gains can result. This is because the temperament for trading would be more secure and less subject to the market wind's whims and sways.

Not all, of course, subscribes to this philosophy. Others swear by the touch and go stop losing, where it simply implies that if the price ever reaches $30, as in our previous case, then the trade will end. For any span of time, there is no discussion of waiting for a close.

Under this scenario, the trader will have better control of his loss number, so his trade would be out every time $30 is reached. That also implies, however, that his odds of getting flushed out of his stop would still be much better than a trader who used the strategy of closing-stop failure.

For me, the way things are handled is not right or wrong. Often it comes down to character and psychology in dealing. I see the folks who love lots of activity are more likely to use the touch-stop method of managing stop losses, while the folks who are a bit more reserved and smoother prefer to wait for further clarification and use the close-stop loss approach as a result.

I used to subscribe to the contact pause since it was the most common and showed the most. But I didn't like the idea that I was still on the right side of the exchange only to lose it when I was pushed out of place. It's almost like a double smack on the cheek. You make a mistake because, in the trading call, you wind up being correct.

That's when the near stop for me came into action, and it performed great in my view so far.

These two methods of managing stop losses are, of course, much preferable to another form of dealing stop-loss, which has no stop losses. Honestly, I can't tell it, but here's my reiteration again, there's still a stop loss, even if it's only a mental price amount. Bear the degree in mind, and you'll need to conduct the escape until it's broken. It is a fight, a war in which any exchange. If a stop-loss is broken, you realize the fight has been lost, but the fighting is always going on as long as you have the capital. Still fail to a halt.

This will be one more thing to remember. Determining the price range for a stop loss needs to make sense from the viewpoint of business research. By what do I mean? In the case of Adam, the $30 price point was calculated simply by the sum Adam was able to sacrifice and by the value of his part. This is not the way it can be, and the scenario was just kept up to demonstrate how the stop-loss could perform.

You should really keep two points in mind with a trade call first. The purchase price, or the amount you are able to pay to share in the stock's prosperity, as well as the stop loss amount calculated by the techniques of market research. In certain situations, citizens turn to scientific analyses to get a stop-loss price. They can extract price ranges from their lines of assistance and opposition and have ears identified as possible stop losses. That is also why I also point out that the task of technical analysis is more of a precision method, whereas that of fundamental analysis will be more of a filtration device to get your fine, worthwhile stocks.

This also ensures you shouldn't have too close a stop while selecting your stop-loss rate. For e.g., in the case of Adam, if his entry price was $40, and there appeared to be a slight amount of help at $38, and Adam was currently preparing his trade for the longer haul, it would be very hard to position his stop at $38. As a rule of thumb, a longer trading time will normally entail a greater loss of the pause. Similarly, if you play longer and miss a bigger rest, the benefits goals would typically be higher too. This is for each exchange to ensure a fair risk-reward ratio.

One thing I've been guilty of in the past was selecting and selecting tighter stop losses, so that helped me to have greater share visibility and thereby gain more money, at least in my opinion! I'd pick a close stop and then genuinely hope the economy doesn't hit that amount. Any of my trades have been so unbelievably organized that I will be in a deal and then out of business within a few minutes, with a few hundred losses to match. This was especially so whilst I was still doing the lack of contact pause. It doesn't make sense to look fine on paper and assume the economy doesn't affect the lack of the end. Also, beginning to calculate the gain right before beginning the exchange is no good. Engaging in mental gymnastics like that will just waste your focus and leave you empty when you need it.

That is why virtually all trades that end up as winners start with the first issue of how much we might lose. All that's on offer is truth and statistics and less optimism and wishful thinking. It's crucial that we perceive things as what they are and not what we expect them to be.

Stock Screeners

These items are so popular these days, with most of them being accessible through web browsers and online. The primary usage of stock screeners will be to have some sort of automatic support while we deal with the boring task of searching out filtering firms.

With only a few mouse clicks, screeners will support a lot in this world with hundreds of thousands of stocks, and we'll have a more accessible shortlist of a handful of hundreds. Okay, it was almost a half-joke, but to be frank, occasionally, you still had to dig around a couple of hundred businesses to get to some deserving of being sold.

Insiders and Institutional Investors

As well as being the hard weights, these guys are also the ones who know most about their businesses. Knowing their records will give us a big leg up for institutional investors when it comes to our investment decisions.

Looking at individual pages documenting those trends and also reading the annual reports to get a sense of who is who and who is doing what would be nice, but it could create too much of a cognitive challenge. Imagine tracking the shortlist of fifty individual securities and maintaining track of insider and retail activity. That pushed the wall toward me.

An easier approach I find for myself would be to use the professional analysts' concept and trust it. The stock price has all caught that which needs to be understood. I keep on board the notion when it comes to tracking products that have already been shortlisted. Yet when it comes to getting the shortlist together, there's simply no moving away from the hard legwork that comes with the foundational research.

For me, fundamental analysis with its regular hard work would guide the way in the development of my monitoring shortlist of stocks; then, technical analysis would offer me the degree of pricing to implement my investing ideas.

Conclusion

I hope this book: Stock Market Investing for Beginners: An Amazing Guide About Stocks on Margin and Penny Stocks, Including Some Wonderful Strategies That Will Help You in the World of the Stock Market has been most useful to you, and with these principles and concepts you can get started in an effective way!

About penny stocks we can say that they are a reasonable means of raising funds to start and grow the business, which is generally used by small businesses and startups, as it is one of the fastest and most effective means of raising capital through the protracted process. Although there can be a considerable gain when trading with penny stocks, as there is enormous volatility in the market, at the same time, there is a considerable risk of losing the significant investment amount even in a short period of time.

About buying on margin can be summed up in one word: LEVERAGE. Just as a company borrows money to invest in its projects, you as an *investor can borrow money and leverage the money you invest.*

You should already know that margin accounts involve risks and are not for every investor. Leverage is a double-edged sword, amplifying losses and gains in equal measure. In fact, one of the definitions of risk is the degree of asset price swing. Since leverage amplifies these swings then, by definition, it increases the risk of your portfolio.

Good luck in your next projects, and thank you for making it to the end of this book!

CPSIA information can be obtained
at www.ICGtesting.com
Printed in the USA
BVHW081011070421
604341BV00006B/790